QUEEN

REX Collections

QUEEN

RAY TEDMAN

Reynolds & Hearn Ltd
London

First published in 2005 by
Reynolds & Hearn Ltd
61a Priory Road
Kew Gardens
Richmond
Surrey TW9 3DH

A CIP catalogue for this book is available from the British Library.

ISBN 1-905287-12-7

Designed by James King.

Printed and bound in Slovenia by
Compass Press Ltd

CONTENTS

1. A ROYAL FAMILY ASSEMBLES

On 29 November 1975 Queen's fifth single 'Bohemian Rhapsody' reached number one in the United Kingdom, where it remained for nine weeks. On 27 December in the same year their fourth album *A Night at the Opera* reached number one in the UK chart. It stayed there for about a year. In the 1999 Music of the Millennium poll, organised by Channel Four and HMV, around 600,000 people voted 'Bohemian Rhapsody' the best song, Queen the second best band after the Beatles and Freddie Mercury (who had died in 1991) sixth-best vocalist (after Elvis Presley, Robbie Williams, Michael Jackson, Frank Sinatra and George Michael).

The group which achieved all of this started its life as Queen on 25 June 1970 with a gig in the city hall, Truro. Brian May and Roger Taylor's group Smile had collapsed after Tim Stafell (a fellow student of Freddie Mercury at Ealing Art College) quit the group. Freddie, who had hung out with the band, convinced May and Taylor that they could put together a stage act with him as lead singer. Mercury (who had changed his name from Bulsara) also pushed hard for the group to change its name. Queen, as he later explained '[is] very regal, it's strong, universal, immediate.' At the very moment of the group's birth it was clear that Freddie's self-belief and vision were the keys to shaping the future megagroup. Three bass players later John Deacon was introduced to May and Taylor by a mutual friend and on 7 July 1971 Deacon's debut with the band completed the line up of the soon-to-be rock gods, who were respectively busy completing an electronics degree (Deacon), a biology degree (Taylor), an astronomy PhD (May), and a graphic arts diploma (Mercury). For the next 12 months not much happened apart from regular gigs, until the group were offered a contract (signed in November 1972) by Trident Productions. This comprised a small wage (£20.00 per week each) plus the chance to record an album at Trident Studios (but only in downtime – largely in the small hours of the morning).

By the end of the year the album was almost finished – but Queen still had no record deal. That was about to change. In April 1973, EMI signed a deal with Trident and Queen's astonishing ride to fame and fortune was under way. The first single and album released in July 1973, 'Keep Yourself Alive' and *Queen,* barely caused a flicker on the chart seismograph.

Although the earth had failed to move, Trident and EMI backed the recording of a new album and in August Queen were back in the studio, recording what was to be *Queen II.* With a big budget for the first time, the group was able to experiment and expand existing ideas. In the words of Brian May, 'We got the overdrive guitars, we built textures. *Queen II* was the music we'd always wanted to play.'

In spite of Queen's success as the supporting band for the winter 1973 Mott the Hoople tour, it took a final twist of fate for the band to reach the charts. Just before the release of the single 'Seven Seas of Rhye', Queen were booked on *Top Of The Pops* as a last-minute substitute for David Bowie. The band 'played' to 10 million viewers on 22 February 1974. In March the single reached number 10, the same month that *Queen II* hit number five in the album charts. The same month Queen began their first headline tour, with Freddie resplendent in his Zandra Rhodes designed white 'eagle suit'.

After problems on their US tour supporting Mott the Hoople, as a result of Brian May's ill-health, the band began recording their third album at Rockfield Studios in June 1974. This was a beautiful residential studio in the Wye Valley near the Welsh market town of Monmouth. From these sessions came the album *Sheer Heart Attack* and the number two single *Killer Queen.* Another UK tour began in October (with the London Rainbow gig selling out in two days), followed by an 11-date European tour. Champagne flowed (donated by Möet and Chandon – mentioned in the first lines of the single), there were parties and limousines – and Trident increased Queen's wages to £60 a week.

Band of brothers 1970.

The band hanging out at Rockfield Studios while working on *Sheer Heart Attack*, June 1975.

Freddie Mercury

Roger Taylor

John Deacon

Next pages: Rockfield Studios 1975.

Freddie Mercury (second left) waiting for his share of the Mott the Hoople cake, 1973. Also (left to right) Ian Hunter, Overend Watts, Morgan Fisher and Roger Taylor.

Freddie and Brian getting it together at London's Rainbow Theatre, 31 March 1974

2. THE REIGN BEGINS

By the beginning of 1975 the band was desperate to escape from the straitjacket of their contract with Trident. After months of wrangling, which had stifled their creativity, a deal was struck in August 1975. Free of Trident's control, Queen turned to Elton John's manager John Reid to manage their ascent to superstardom.

In August, as if in celebration of their new-found independence, Queen started studio work on the album *A Night at the Opera*. Mercury spoke of his eagerness to 'experiment' and 'go to extremes'. May's take was 'We thought, this time, we are really going for it – this can be our *Sgt. Pepper*.' The track 'Bohemian Rhapsody' epitomised Queen's new freedom to be 'wonderfully weird'. The six-minute composition took three weeks to record, including seven twelve-hour days for the 180-voice chorale. Selected by the band as the single release from the album, their record label EMI were nonplussed. No radio station would play such a long track. Then DJ Kenny Everett played the track 14 times in one weekend on London's Capital Radio. As EMI marketing manager Paul Watts said 'From the very minute you heard it on the radio you just *knew*.'

The clincher was the video, shot on a soundstage at Elstree Studios over two days for the then-enormous sum of £4000. With an opening sequence echoing the iconic Mick Rock portrait from *Queen 2* and costumes designed by Zandra Rhodes, the video premiered on *Top Of The Pops* on 20 November 1975. On 29 November 'Bohemian Rhapsody' hit number one in the UK. On 27 December *A Night at the Opera* reached number one in the UK album charts, a day after Queen's BBC Radio 1/BBC1 simulcast from London's Hammersmith Odeon. In January 1976 the album and the single were released in the US, peaking at number four and number nine respectively. In September of the same year Queen played to 150,000 fans at a free concert in Hyde Park. The stadium rock era was beginning.

The band's fifth album *A Day at the Races* was released in the UK and the US in December, topping the UK chart in January 1977, and reaching number five in the US the following month. Yet, even as the band appeared unstoppable, things were changing. Queen had been scheduled to appear on ITV's *Today* show in autumn 1976, but cancelled at the last moment. Their last-minute replacements were the Sex Pistols, whose foul-mouthed exchanges with host Bill Grundy thrust punk rock centre stage. In June 1977, the Pistols' 'God Save the Queen' was *de facto* number one during the Royal Jubilee.

Freddie and John Reid (right) at Kempton Park race course for the launch of *A Day at the Races* October 1976.

This spread and overleaf: the 1976 Hyde Park concert.

Members of the board

Brian deep in thought in the studio. *Bohemian Rhapsody*
took three weeks to record.

Are these for us? Queen receives the BPI (later Brit) award for 'Bohemian Rhapsody' in 1977. The shared the award with Procul Harum and 'A Whiter Shade of Pale'.

3. THEIR MAJESTY'S PLEASURE

Back at planet Queen the road to excess was open. The cheques had started flowing in while the band were recording *A Night at the Opera*. Now there were vast new stage sets and a state-of-the art lighting rig, increasingly elaborate costumes and champagne by the truck load. Freddie indulged in increasingly extravagant retail therapy. Then the band achieved yet another award from the trophy cabinet of rock stardom – tax exile. Nevertheless, their work rate remained high. In January 1977 they began a US tour, including New York's Madison Square Gardens. The following May a 19-date European tour kicked off, culminating in two nights in London's Earls Court Arena. There was a further US tour in November.

Meanwhile the band were recording their next album, *News of the World*. Brian May announced that Queen

were getting back to basics. Certainly the double A-side single 'We Are the Champions/We Will Rock You' released in October 1977 had a certain footstomping, hand-waving directness. The single reached number two in the UK and number four in the US. The album peaked at number four in the UK while the Sex Pistols' *Never Mind the Bollocks* captured the number one spot. Changes were underway at the helm of the Queen enterprise. John Reid departed with a pay-off and the band formed its own management company. This resulted in a new multi-million deal with EMI. Mercury, Taylor, Deacon and May became the highest paid company directors in the United Kingdom, picking up £690,000 each in 1978-9.

April 1978 saw the start of another Queen European tour, and October a new US tour. In May, work started

on *Jazz*, their seventh album. The double A-side single 'Bicycle Race/Fat Bottomed Girls' was released in October, promoted in part by a video of 65 naked young women in a bicycle race. The album was launched at a party at the Fairmont Hotel in New Orleans – an event which became a byword for extravagance and excess. Room after room was filled with strippers, drag acts, prostitutes and other assorted freaks offering anything from nude wrestling in baths of liver to plates of cocaine and queues for blowjobs in the toilets. Brian May said later 'We were always trying to get to a place that had never been reached before and excess is part of that.' So successful was the party that the album never got played. Although creatively it seemed to be marking time, *Jazz* reached number two in the UK and number four in the US.

'We always said that we wanted to be the biggest band in the world. Unashamedly, that was the object of the enterprise. What else are you going to say – we'd like to be fourth biggest?' said Roger Taylor. The band's apparently relentless journey to world domination continued in 1979 with tours to Europe, Japan, Ireland and the UK, the release of *Killer*, a double live album, and work on the new album *The Game*. Freddie's neo-Elvis Presley song 'Crazy Little Thing Called Love' was released in the UK in October, reaching number two in the UK.

A new look for the 1979 tour.

Manchester 1979.

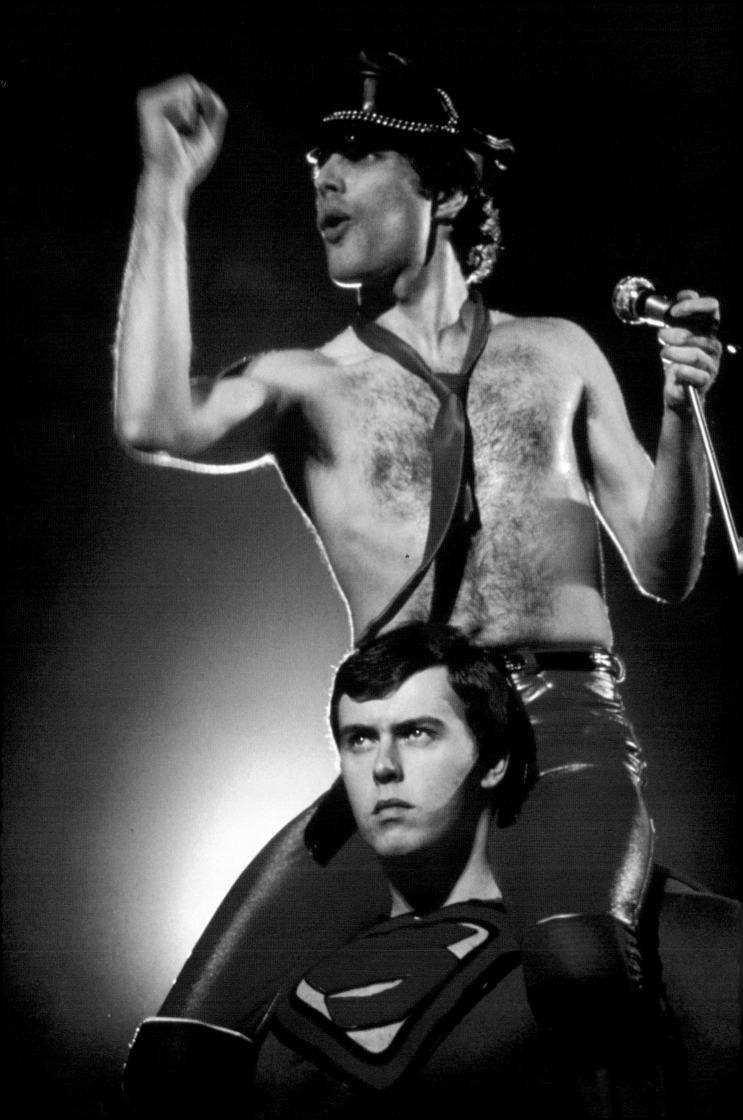

4. GLOBAL POWER

On 4 May 1979 Conservative Party leader Margaret Thatcher became Britain's first woman prime minister. Over the next decade the grocer's daughter from Grantham achieved domination of her party and the country she ruled. As the clocks ticked past midnight on 31 December 1979, ushering in the 1980s, Queen were entering the decade that brought their apotheosis. A fantasy maybe, but it's easy to think of Mrs Thatcher listening to 'We Are the Champions' and singing along with the line 'no time for losers'.

In February 1980 'Crazy Little Thing Called Love' gave Queen their first number one US single. *The Game* was released in the UK in June, hitting the number one album spot in July. The band began their three-month North American tour in the same month. *The Game* became US number one album in September and 'Another One Bites the Dust' became US number one single in October. In the face of relentless success, Freddie's behaviour was sometimes erratic. Sporting his new short haircut and moustache, he asked his audience in Chicago if he should keep the moustache. 'Do you say no? Fuck off!' He arrived on stage at Madison Square Garden extremely late, dowsing the front row with a magnum of champagne and proclaiming that the audience were 'all cunts'. Freddie's later explanation of his behaviour as 'irony' did not cut much ice.

Also, during 1980, Queen recorded the soundtrack for the Dino de Laurentis film *Flash Gordon*. In the words of Daryl Easlea, '…half an hour or so of crashing, banging and walloping to accompany a movie remake of the 1930s US comic strip and serial. *Flash Gordon* is the album that reinforces a hardcore Queen fan's love of the band and ensures that those who despise the group do

so with renewed passion.' By the end of 1980 the band had sold 45 million albums and 25 million singles worldwide.

If 1980 had been good, then 1981 was magnificent. In February the band was in Tokyo for a five-concert sell out. March saw stadium rock reach new heights in the first leg of Queen's South American tour. The Morumbi Stadium in São Paulo, Brazil set a world record of 131,000 paying customers on the first night. Over 250,000 people heard the band over two nights. Work started on the next album in May at Queen's Mountain Studios in Montreux. Near neighbour David Bowie was introduced to the group, resulting in the jointly written single 'Under Pressure'. Bowie's comment on the meeting of egos was 'It was, er, peculiar.' 'Under Pressure' made it to number one in the UK, and also Argentina, where it remained throughout the Falklands war.

As a grand finale to the year, the album *Queen's Greatest Hits* was released, together with a video and a book. In November the album, the single 'Under Pressure' and the video *Queen's Greatest Flix* topped the UK listings simultaneously – another first for Queen. They were now a global brand. The question was – what did a global brand do next? Freddie's answer was a disco album. Supported by John Deacon, whose 'Another One Bites the Dust' had given the group their second US number one, *Hot Space* emerged in May 1982, clearly showing the ambivalence of Roger Taylor and Brian May to the project. An uneasy potpourri of funk mixed with typical Queen products such as 'Las Palabras de Amor', the album peaked at number four in the UK while the single 'Body Language' struggled to number 25.

Following their normal pattern, in support of the album Queen commenced a worldwide tour in April 1982 with a concert in Gothenburg, Sweden. The group were in for a rude shock. Experimentation was not what their fans wanted. Backing groups such as Bow Wow Wow and The Teardrop Explodes were mercilessly bottled. At the 5 June Milton Keynes Bowl concert in the UK Freddie was forced to explain to the crowd 'Now most of you know we've got some new sounds out in the last week and for what it's worth we're going to do a few songs in the black/funk category, whatever you call it. That doesn't mean we've lost our rock 'n' roll feel, OK. I mean it's only a bloody record.'

The US leg of the tour (34 shows at 30 venues over eight weeks) was, it turned out, Queen's last American foray. They had changed but the audiences wanted the old Queen, not Freddie in his short-haired, moustachioed persona. Billy Squier, one of Queen's support acts, summed it up. 'When people over here like a band they expect certain things from you. Fred's image makeover, with its social implications, and the abrupt musical shift towards disco were two radical departures from what American audiences expected.'

The tour ended with a series of November dates in Japan. If 1981 had been their apogee then 1982 seemed to be their nadir. The band decided to take a year off.

Freddie Mercury and his cat 1980.

Play the Game 1980.

Elton John and Freddie Mercury wearing a *Flash Gordon* t-shirt.
Queen provided half an hour of 'crashing, banging and walloping'
to accompany the film.

5. TROUBLED TIMES

The band also took a year off from each other. As well as enjoying the fringe benefits of rock millionairedom, both Brian and Freddie embarked on solo projects, Brian on *Star Fleet Project* and Freddie on his Giorgio Moroder produced album *Mr Bad Guy*, which also yielded the single 'Love Kills'.

As with all holidays, eventually it was time to go back to work. Freddie, Roger, John and Brian packed away their vacation clothes and clocked in at LA's Record Plant in September 1983. Completed at Giorgio Moroder's Munich Musicland studio, *The Works* yielded four singles including 'Radio Ga Ga' and 'I Want to Break Free'. Although it only reached number two in the UK, the album reached number one in 19 countries. Both singles yielded memorable videos – 'Radio Ga Ga' for the massed double handclap section and 'I Want to Be Free' for the site of the whole band in drag. In typical heavy-handed manner, MTV refused to show the video in the US – presumably to prevent an epidemic of cross-dressing (presumably with false moustaches). Although the album reached number two in the UK, it only struggled to number 23 in the US.

Once again Queen had an album to promote. In May 1984 the band played the Swiss Golden Rose Pop Festival, reaching a TV audience of 350 million. In August the European tour began, ending in Vienna at the end of September. At the same time the video of the *We Will Rock You* concert was number one in the UK. Then the band managed to snatch defeat from the jaws of victory by playing seven shows at Sun City in South Africa, breaking a United Nations cultural boycott and ending up on a UN blacklist. Planet Queen had collided with reality.

There was more trouble when Queen appeared at the Rock in Rio festival. 'I Want to Break Free' had become a protest song against the Brazilian regime and the crowd did not appreciate Freddie's cross-dressing. 'I don't know why they got so excited about me dressing up as a woman. There are lots of transvestites here' was Freddie's comment. In the same interview Freddie said that he would have liked to have been included in the Band Aid single 'Do They Know It's Christmas?'. 'I don't know if they would have had me anyway because I'm a bit old. I'm just an old slag who gets up in the morning, scratches his head and wonders who he wants to fuck.'

Elton John and Freddie Mercury

Freddie dressing down in Rio 1985.

6. QUEEN AID

Help was at hand – in the form of that latter-day saint Bob Geldof. Geldof was organising a vast charity event – Live Aid, with simultaneous concerts at London's Wembley Stadium and Philadelphia's JFK Stadium, on 13 July 1985. The event, which was to raise money for the Ethiopian famine, also relaunched Queen. Of all the bands appearing, only Queen had rehearsed properly, hiring London's Shaw Theatre for a week before the show. Freddie was in his element and the set of 'Bohemian Rhapsody', 'Radio Ga Ga', 'Hammer to Fall', 'Crazy Little Thing Called Love', 'We Will Rock You' and 'We Are the Champions' rocked the stadium and the 1.5 billion viewers. As David Grohl (later a member of Nirvana) said 'Everybody played that gig and Queen smoked 'em all. They walked away being the greatest band you'd ever seen in your life.'

The hard-headed businessman Roger Taylor said to reporters before the event, 'Of course, it is a wonderful cause and will make a pot of money for that wonderful cause. But make no mistake. We're doing it for our own glory as well.' He was right. Following the concert, Queen record sales rose five-fold while Mr Bad Guy re-entered the charts. Live Aid over, the band scattered, coming together later in the year to work on the soundtrack for the film Highlander starring Christopher Lambert and Sean Connery. In September, Freddie celebrated his 39th birthday with a black and white drag ball at Old Mrs Henderson's in Munich. The band's single One Vision was released in November, reaching number seven in the UK and featuring on the soundtrack of the movie Iron Eagle. In December, a limited edition

boxed set containing every album by Queen was released, titled The Complete Works.

Early in 1986 the band was back in the studio working on the soundtrack for Highlander and the music formed the backbone of the album A Kind of Magic, released in May 1986. The single of the same title released in March reached number three in the UK and number one in 35 other countries, while the album reached number one and went double-platinum. In May, Freddie released his fourth single 'Time', the title theme from a stage musical starring Cliff Richard. On 7 June the band embarked on the Magic tour with a concert at AIK Stockholm's football stadium in Sweden. Over the next two months they performed in front of one million fans, including gigs in Budapest, Paris and London's Wembley, culminating in their last live gig together in front of an audience of 120,000 at the Knebworth Festival on 9 August. Freddie's closing words were 'Thank you, you beautiful people. Good night, sweet dreams. We love you.'

That evening, although the Queen brand was set to endure, Queen the band, the supreme live performance group, finally yielded to the internal strains over money, creative issues and the years of demanding tours. There would be two more studio albums but no more live performances. The band's single, released in September, had a strange resonance – 'Who Wants to Live Forever?'. To soften the blow, the release of Live Magic, their definitive live album in December 1986, revealed the band at the height of their powers – the biggest rock band on earth.

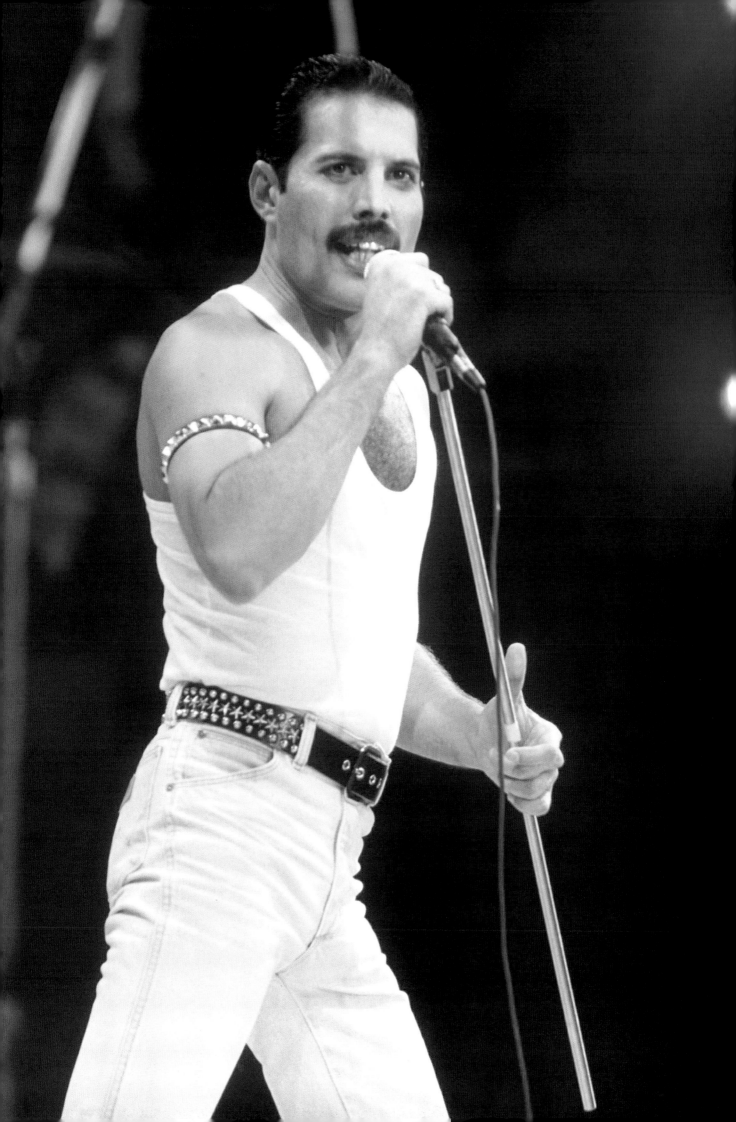

A princess chats to two Queens

The stadium rocks – the Wembley crowd.

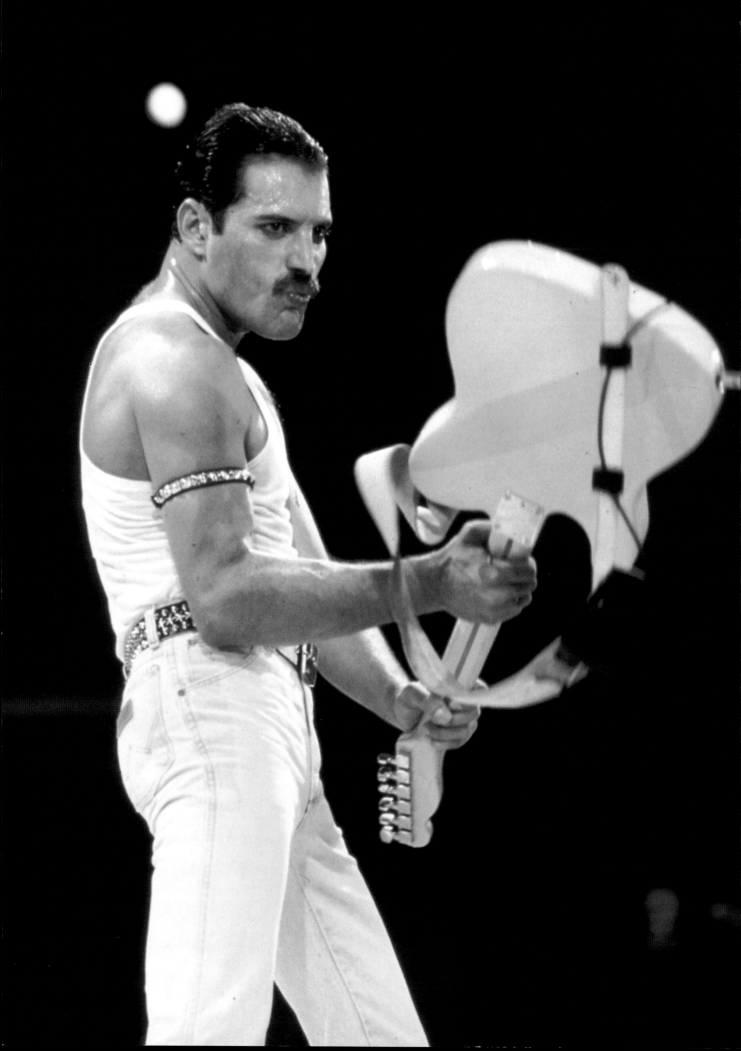

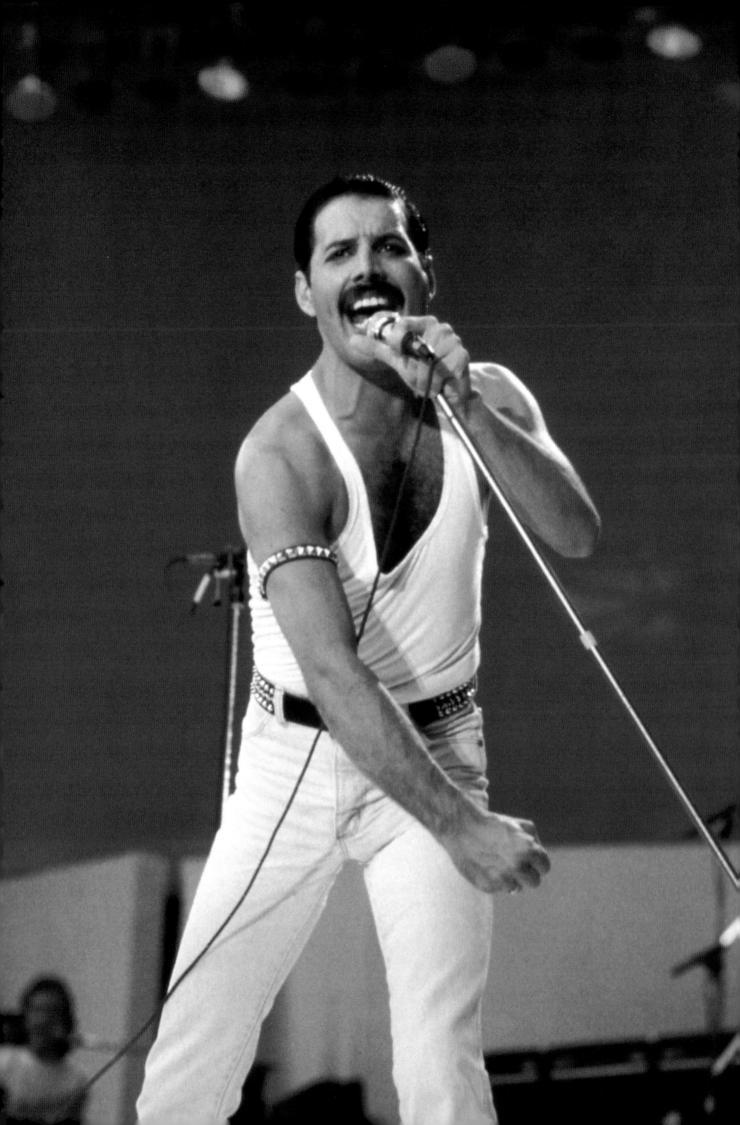

Freddie backstage at Live Aid with Wayne Sleep and Elton John.

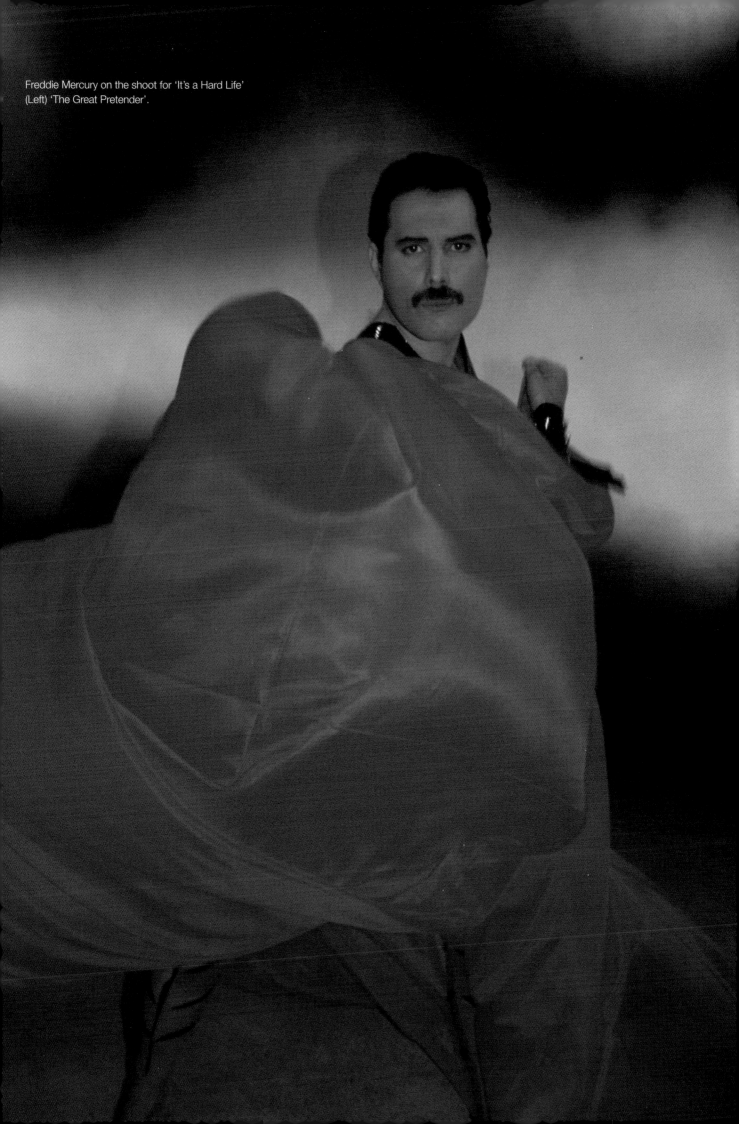

Freddie Mercury on the shoot for 'It's a Hard Life'
(Left) 'The Great Pretender'.

Video for 'It's a Hard Life'.

Freddie Mercury, Dublin 1986.

Dublin July 1986

Next pages; Wembley, 1986.

Wembley 14 July 1986.

Steady Freddie! Christopher Lambert, star of *Highlander*, engages with Freddie during the shooting of the video for 'A Kind of Magic'.

'The Miracle' in 1989.

Pantomime villains. Debbie Leng is the helpless victim during the filming for *The Miracle* in 1989.

Brian May and Freddie Mercury during the
filming of 'The Invisible Man' video 1989.

7. THE KING IS DEAD

The hiatus in the band's activities finally gave Freddie time to move into his house, Garden Lodge, in Kensington. Accompanying him, among others, were his live-in lover Jim Hutton and his two adored cats. Freddie's sexuality had been a matter of intense discussion for many years. In his glam rock days his appearance and behaviour were no more camp than many notoriously straight artistes. Furthermore, he had a long-term girlfriend, Mary Austin. But, as the Queen years passed by, it became clear that Freddie was not straight. Or, indeed, exclusively gay. Perhaps, given his appetites, omnisexual is the best term.

HIV and AIDS had arrived on the radar in the mid-1980s. The death of American film star Rock Hudson in October 1985 sparked off intense public awareness – and fear of the illness. Aware of his vulnerability, Freddie had an AIDS test in 1985, which proved negative. But Mercury, the messenger of the gods, had become Icarus. His meeting with the sun was probably around Easter 1987, when he was diagnosed as HIV positive and began his long fall to earth.

Freddie's drive to create seemed as strong as ever. He worked with producer Mike Moran on a cover version of the Platters' hit 'The Great Pretender'. With the wordless 'Exercises in Free Love' as the B-side, the single reached number four – his most successful solo single in the UK. Later in the year Freddie formed an unlikely alliance with Spanish opera diva Montserrat Caballe, accompanying her on the piano at Covent Garden as she sang her version of 'Exercises in Free Love'. The Catalan diva seemed to take a real shine to Freddie, and, at a post-performance dinner at Garden Lodge,

she asked him and Mike Moran if they would write a piece about Barcelona. 'Of course' said Freddie, promptly forgetting about it

As Freddie was coming to terms with his diagnosis, suddenly Caballe was calling him from around the world asking how he was getting on with the song. Freddie realised he'd have to deliver. Caballe's demands enabled him to throw himself into his work and focus on getting on with life. 'Barcelona' was written in short order by Freddie and Moran. The single was recorded in London with 'Exercises in Free Love' as the B-side. In May, Freddie and Montserrat Caballe headlined at the Ku Club in Ibiza performing 'Barcelona' live. When the single was released in Spain in September it sold over 10,000 copies in the first three hours.

Work continued on a Caballe/Mercury album, with a break for another Freddie birthday party at his friend Tony Pike's hotel in Ibiza. Seven hundred guests enjoyed an evening flowing with champagne, flamenco and fantasy dancers, rounded off with a dramatic firework display. Sadly, no one had any room for the two-metre long cake. Freddie still wasn't ready to go public about his condition. In November, in an interview with a women's magazine, he said 'Yes I did have an AIDS test, and I'm fine.'

In January 1988 the band re-assembled to start work on their first studio album for three years. Freddie, although as driven as ever, tired easily and the album was to take almost a year to record. In the meantime the *Barcelona* album was still being finished. The album was due to be released in mid-October, but before that Freddie and Montserrat performed two tracks from the album as the finale of a vast open-air concert in

Freddie shaves off his moustache for 'The Great Pretender' video.

Relaxing without moustache in Ibiza, Spain, 1987.

Barcelona with the Barcelona Opera house orchestra and choir. Although the performance was supposed to be live, at the last moment Freddie insisted that Montserrat and he should mime to a voice track. In spite of some technical problems the whole performance was, nonetheless, magical.

Queen's 13th album, *The Miracle,* was released in May 1989, as was the single 'I Want It All'. The album reached number one in the UK, while the single peaked at number three. Four more singles from the album were released through the year: 'Breakthru', 'The Invisible Man', 'Scandal' and 'The Miracle'. The steady release of singles kept Queen in the public eye while they recorded what was to be their last album in Switzerland and London. Freddie's illness meant that recording stretched over the whole of 1990. In February of that year, Queen received the Outstanding Contribution to British Music trophy at the Brit awards. Freddie's health continued to worsen. Finally, in early January 1991, he told his fellow band members that he was dying of AIDS. 'You probably realize what my problem is. Well that's it, and I don't want it to be known. I don't want to talk about it. I just want to get on and work until I can't work any more.'

On 26 January the new single 'Innuendo' entered the UK singles chart at number one. The album of the same name was released in February. It entered the UK chart at number one. In the US it reached number 30. In May the single 'Headlong' was released, reaching number 14 in the UK. The single 'The Show Must Go On' reached number 16 in the same year. On 9 November *Greatest Hits II* entered the UK chart at number one. On 24 November 1991, Freddie Mercury died at Garden Lodge, of complications from AIDS. He was 45. In death Freddie was able to be frank with his public. A brief statement read 'Freddie Mercury died peacefully this evening at his home. His death was the result of bronchopneumonia, brought on by AIDS.' The announcement of the death brought a flood of fans to the house, together with hundreds of floral tributes. Three days later Mercury was cremated at a private ceremony. A week later, in a TV interview, Roger Taylor and Brian May said that the remaining members of the band hoped to plan a tribute to Freddie – perhaps in the form of a live concert.

'Bohemian Rhapsody' was re-released on 9 December as a double A-side with the unreleased 'These Are the Days of Our Lives'. It swept into the chart

The rock star and the Diva. Freddie
and Montserrat Caballe in 1987.

Montserrat and Freddie perform 'Barcelona' in Barcelona, October 1988.

at number one, becoming the second bestselling single of 1991. All royalties from the disc were donated to the Terrence Higgins Trust.

On 20 April 1992 the Freddie Mercury Tribute Concert for Aids Awareness was staged at London's Wembley Stadium featuring (among others) George Michael, Guns 'n' Roses, Roger Daltrey, Elton John, David Bowie, Annie Lennox, Paul Young, Mick Ronson and Liza Minnelli. With a worldwide TV audience of nearly a billion it was the biggest music event since Live Aid. As well as a memorial for Mercury, the concert was an AIDS awareness day with all profits going to charity. Shortly after the tribute, the three remaining members of Queen announced that they were to disband.

There was some unfinished business. In late November 1992 an album of Freddie solo tracks *The Freddie Mercury Album* charted at number four. There were reissues of *The Great Pretender* and *In My Defence*, and in July 1993 a track from the solo album *Mr Bad Guy* 'Living on My Own' reached number one in the singles chart, Mercury's first solo number one in the UK.

There remained enough recorded material for a final Queen album. After a considerable amount of tinkering by the remaining band members, *Made in Heaven* was released in November 1995, shooting straight to number one and staying in the top five throughout Christmas. The album was 'Dedicated to the immortal spirit of Freddie Mercury'. Mercury's view may have been different. When asked how he would like people to remember him professionally he said 'Dead and gone? It's up to them. When I'm dead who cares? I don't.'

'The Great Pretender' video 1987.

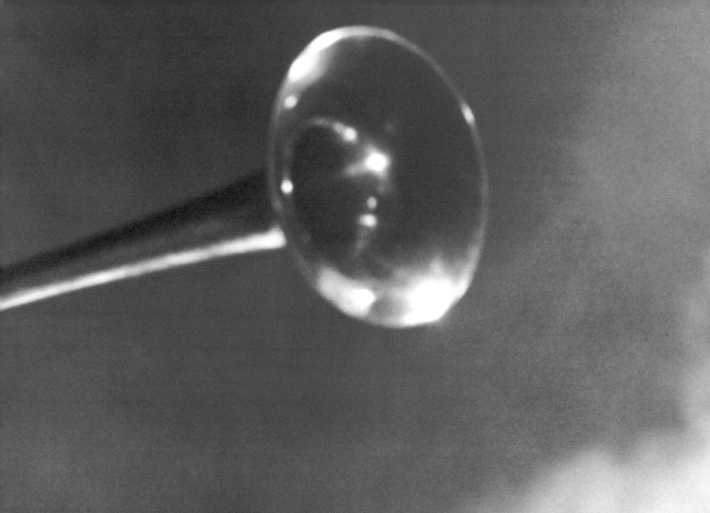

'The Great Pretender' video, 1987.

Freddie Mercury and Debbie Ash in 'The Great Pretender' video, 1987.

The band at the 1990 Brits, where they received an award for their outstanding contribution to the British music industry.

(Top): Freddie with Bob Geldof, and (bottom) with David Gilmour

Freddie Mercury's funeral, London, November 1991.

Flowers left by fans at the door of Freddie's home Garden Lodge after his death.

Brian May and Liza Minnelli at the Freddie Mercury Tribute Concert,
Wembley Stadium 1992.

Lisa Stansfield, George Michael and Brian May.

Roger Taylor, Brian May and Roger Daltrey.

Annie Lennox and David Bowie.

Elton John and Axl Rose of Guns 'n' Roses show respect.

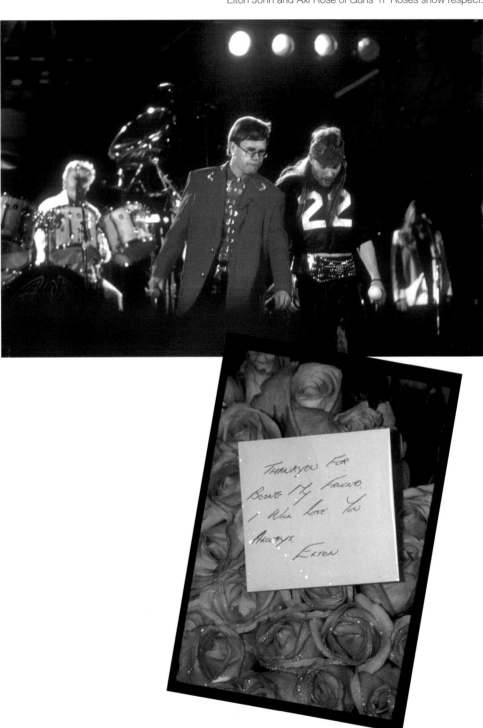

8. POST REGNUM

The world wasn't going to forget. In May 1994 'Living on My Own' won the International Hit of the Year at the Ivor Novello Awards. In March 1996 *Made in Heaven* was certified as a US gold album, while in June 'Let Me Live' entered the UK singles chart at number nine. In 1997 *Made in Heaven* was certified as four-time platinum in the UK, while the compilation album *Queen Rocks* reached number seven in the UK.

In 1999 Freddie featured on a UK postage stamp – one of a set celebrating the end of the millennium and the beginning of the next. In May 2002 *We Will Rock You*, a musical based on Queen songs, opened at London's Dominion theatre. Productions also opened in Australia and Las Vegas. At the Royal Golden Jubilee concert held at Buckingham Palace, Brian May kicked off the evening by playing 'God Save the Queen' on the roof of the palace. In November of the same year Brian collected an honorary doctorate in science from the University of Hertfordshire.

In December 2004 came the announcement that reports of Queen's demise had been greatly exaggerated. A new tour was announced. Roger Taylor and Brian May would be joined by bass player Danny Miranda (John Deacon having declined to take part). The new singer would be ex-Free and Bad Company frontman Paul Rodgers.

The tour kicked off with a fan club only show at London's Brixton Academy, ending in Japan after a 41 show tour, including two in the US. Audience numbers showed that Queen remained a potent brand. On 28 September 2005 Sony Ericsson announced the result of a worldwide poll of 700,000 music fans. 'We Are the Champions' was voted the world's favourite song.

Brian May plays at the Queen's Golden Jubilee Party at the Palace, June 2002.

Roger Taylor and Brian May with the London cast of *We Will Rock You* after the 1000th performance in January 2005.

Paul Rodgers, Roger Taylor and Brian May give it up at 'Queen in Concert' in London's Hyde Park, 15 July 2005.

'I'm not replacing Freddie – nobody could. He's a completely different kind of singer and songwriter. That's why we're Queen with Paul Rodgers.'

ACKNOWLEDGEMENTS

Thanks to: Andy Godfrey, Marcus Hearn, Glen Marks and everyone at Rex Features, Richard Reynolds and Ulrike Steiner-Tedman.

Special thanks are due to David Pratt, for tracking down so many unseen images.

Photographer credits
(all references are by page numbers)

Eugene Adebari 47-49, 124
Brendan Beirne 75, 76-77
Andre Csillag 8-15,18-19, 22, 23, 26-27,28-29, 40,141,142, 143 (top),145
Clive Dixon 98-99, 135
Everett Collection 16-17,
Harry Goodwin 5,7
Fraser Gray 58-59
Jonathan Hordle 44, 45, 147
Steve Joester 22
Nils Jorgensen 86-97, 143 (bottom)
Linda Matlow 62-63
Mark Mawson 102-103
Frederico Mendes 85
Gary Merrin 41
Ilpo Musto 79, 80
Brian Rasic front cover, 2
Rex Features 30-5, 30-31,37, 38-39, 42, 46, 50-51, 52-53, 64-65, 70-71, 78-79, 136, 139, 158-159
Mick Rock 20, 21, 36, 43
Sheila Rock 68-69
Richard Young 54-57, 60-61, 72-73, 74, 81-83, 100-101, 104-123, 125-134, 137,138,140,146, 148-157